MW01625589

Special dedication to the little ones
of the Bacaron family.

Special thanks to
Yoga Academy for the spiritual guidance

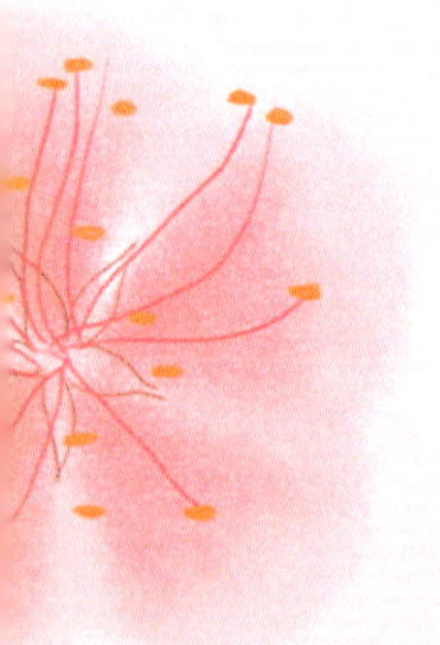

ISBN-978-0-578-71801-9

© Copyright 2020 Hannah Cherise Bacaron

All Rights Reserved

This publication may not be reproduced in whole or in part by any means whatsoever without written permission from the copyright owners.

Permission is never granted for commercial purposes.

This book belongs to:

Your heart respects the entire universe.

Allow your heart to love all living beings
and non-living beings

Do not hold grudges and forgive everyone.

Let yourself be full of positive energy.

Let go of negative energy.

Feel whole and complete.

Remind yourself that you can do anything and everything you set out to do.

Nothing is impossible when you awaken your heart's potential.

Live with peace and harmony.

Posture 1:

One-Legged King Pigeon Pose II
Sanskrit: Eka pada rajakapota

Posture 2:

Camel Pose
Sanskrit: Ushtrasana

Posture 3:

Reclined Lotus Pose
Sanskrit: Supta Padamasana

Posture 4:

Upward-Facing Dog Pose
Sanskrit: Urdhva Mukha Svanasana

Posture 5:

Tree Pose Variation
Sanskrit: Vrksasana

Posture 6:

King Dancer Pose
Sanskrit: Natarajasana

Posture 7:

Handstand
Sanskrit: Adho Mukha Vrksasana

Posture 8:

Bow Pose
Sanskrit: Dhanurasana

Posture 9:

Half Lotus Toe Balance Pose
Sanskrit: Padangustha Padma Utkatasana

Made in the USA
Monee, IL
13 August 2020

38219455R00017